AFTER PUSHKIN

AFTER PUSHKIN

*Versions of the poems of
Alexander Sergeevich Pushkin
by contemporary poets*

Edited and introduced by
ELAINE FEINSTEIN

Preface by
MARITA CRAWLEY

Drawings by Alexander Pushkin

Carcanet Press Ltd

The Folio Society
1999

First published in paperback in 1999 by

CARCANET PRESS LTD
CONAVON COURT
BLACKFRIAR STREET
MANCHESTER M3 5BQ

in association with

THE FOLIO SOCIETY LTD
44 EAGLE STREET
LONDON WCIR 4FS

A CIP catalogue record for this book
is available from the British Library
ISBN 1 85754 444 7

Set in Photina at The Folio Society. Printed in
Great Britain by Butler and Tanner Ltd,
Frome, on Caxton Wove paper

CONTENTS

5

PREFACE

Marita Crawley

Marita Crawley is Chairman of The British Pushkin Bicentennial Trust and a great-great-great-granddaughter of Alexander Pushkin

The idea for this book came from a question. How do you convince the English-speaking public that Pushkin's genius is as great as the Russians claim? In a perfect world, poems would be translated by poets. After all, Shakespeare was translated into Russian by Pasternak. So I thought: what about asking a number of our best living poets to 'translate' some Pushkin poems, or rather to make 'poems' out of Pushkin translations? The idea seemed unbelievably exciting. I was only afraid the poets would not share my enthusiasm.

I was wrong. Ted Hughes's instantaneous response was: 'I would love to have a go. We owe Pushkin so much.' And Seamus Heaney's was: 'I've so much to do but how can I resist?' With this reaction it was perhaps not surprising that The Folio Society, to whom in my eagerness I happened to mention it, immediately said they would like to publish the book even though it was far from their normal kind of venture.

The poetry of Pushkin is deceptively simple. The sound, meaning, rhythm of every word is so unwaveringly apt. The thought of doing justice to any poet in another language, let alone Pushkin, is truly daunting. Pushkin himself called translators 'the post-horses of enlightenment', and, fortunately, undaunted translators have given us many celebrated translations. In this book however, for the first time, we have Pushkin's extraordinary poetry rendered by some of our best poets. So much opera and music has blossomed from Pushkin's bough, as much as from Shakespeare's, and it is through this medium that he has become best known in the West. Perhaps this little volume of a poet's poetry, translated by poets, will help us understand the supreme place that Pushkin holds in Russia.

INTRODUCTION

The Folio Society, fired by the enthusiasm of Marita Crawley, is marking this year's bicentenary of the birth of Alexander Sergeevich Pushkin by bringing out a collection of his poems translated by contemporary poets.

Russians regard Pushkin as the fountainhead of literature. His poems have accompanied prisoners into Tsarist gaols and the Communist Gulag equally. All the Russian writers Western readers have taken to their heart have recorded their debts to him, from his friend Gogol—to whom Pushkin, with prodigal generosity, gave the plots of *Dead Souls* and *The Inspector General*—through Tolstoy, Turgenev, Dostoevsky and the greatest poets of the twentieth century. Yet his work is still known in the West mainly through the operas of Tchaikovsky, Mussorgsky, and Rimsky-Korsakov.

Unlike Shakespeare, who has gone into so many languages with ease, the miraculous lucidity of Pushkin's language has always made him peculiarly resistant to translation. He uses little imagery, relying instead on an effortless, colloquial vigour and an extraordinary felicity of form. This felicity is hard to capture without the Russian case structure, which preserves a clear meaning wherever words are placed in a line of verse; English, particularly, is a language which is uncomfortable with the least distortion of natural word order; and without his shapeliness, Pushkin can sound pretty flat in English.

For all these difficulties, there have been successful translators. Both Charles Johnstone and James E. Falen have made ingeniously readable versions of *Eugene Onegin*. A. D. P. Briggs has brought out an excellent collection of Pushkin's lyrics, and Antony Wood has translated (with great charm) *The Little Tragedies*, a version of *Boris Godunov* and a book of lyrics. None of these translators has been represented in this book, however, which has a different rubric: to involve contemporary *poets* in the task of bringing Pushkin over into English.

Those successfully inveigled into trying to do so come from around the globe: New Zealand and the United States, Ireland, Scotland and Wales as well as England, women and men, and of widely different generations. All have their own, often idiosyncratic, voices. They were encouraged to make an English poem out of the material supplied, and to take what risks they needed to do so. For the most part they had no Russian, though Edwin Morgan was able to translate directly from his own complete text of Pushkin. Some had a friendly Russian scholar able to read the texts aloud. Eavan Boland and Louise Gluck were offered transliterations, stress patterns and word-for-word literals by Antony Wood.

Ted Hughes in the last months of his life collaborated over a period of days with Daniel Weissbort on 'The Prophet'. This is a poem, recognisably based on lines from Isaiah, in which Pushkin speaks of the poet as a man whose body has been physically torn open to have the fire of truth put inside by the hand of God. It was a poem that made Pushkin an iconic figure, both for those who opposed the Tsar, and those who opposed the Soviet regime. Here, the poem reads as freshly as if written in our own time. It is something of a mystery of collaboration that Hughes's version of 'The Prophet', which adheres fairly closely to the vocabulary of Weissbort's literal version, nevertheless has the unmistakable vehemence of Hughes in its rhythms.

There were very disparate approaches to translation and my editorial problem was to see that, even as I urged poets to write poems almost as if they were writing their own, Pushkin was not altogether lost in the process. I realised at the outset it would be foolish to clamp poets into Pushkin's rhythms and rhymes, though Seamus Heaney managed to remain entirely colloquial in his lovely version of 'Arion' while keeping a sense of Pushkin's shape.

Rhyme as such turned out to be less of a problem than I had expected. Pushkin's 'Tsar Nikita and His Forty Daughters' is a romp about forty princesses born without sexual organs. Since it uses short lines of insistent rhyming couplets, the poem presents a translator with horrendous problems, but Ranjit Bolt has a gift for ingenious rhyme and Pushkin comes across brilliantly very much in his own form. Carol Ann Duffy kept part-rhymes and assonances sufficient to signal the structure of the original poem while maintaining her own flippant assurance.

There was never going to be an easy line to draw, as I realised on my first reading of Allen Curnow, whose modernist open verse certainly did not look like Pushkin on the page, but whose lyricism was unmistakable. Vocabulary and anachronism involved rather more delicate editorial decisions. I wanted the poets to write in their own vernacular, as Pushkin had so magnificently established spoken Russian as the language of poetry. The very idiom of contemporary poetry in English is made up of phrases altogether anachronistic to Pushkin's time, and I am well aware of the freedoms taken in, say, Ruth Padel's exuberant version of Tatyana's letter to Eugene Onegin. Dannie Abse added an entirely new verse of his own to Pushkin's squib about Aglaya, the promiscuous wife of General Davydov. I solved that particular problem with a footnote and a version of my own.

'The Bronze Horseman' is a poem I particularly wanted to be in the book. It is an extraordinary *tour de force*, capable of as many readings as the critics who have engaged with it. It opens with a paean to the frozen majesty of St Petersburg, an unmistakable rebuke to the great Polish poet and patriot Mickiewicz, who dared to mock the city of his exile. The description of the flood which wrecked the city in the 1820s has a more compassionate motif. Pushkin catches both the drama of waves crashing through windows, and the pathos of pedlars' trays floating on the waters. At the centre of the story is poor Yevgeny, a clerk who dreams of marriage to his lovely Parasha. His misery at finding her house washed away sends him mad, and leads him to arraign the great Falconet statue of Peter the Great, the Tsar who built his capital below sea-level. Most readers will remember Yevgeny's hallucination that the statue pursues him to his death, the metal hooves clattering on the cobbles of St Petersburg streets. Charles Tomlinson translates the first section of the poem with quiet precision; Carol Rumens's poem, in contrast, is a *jeu d'esprit* of the present day which takes off from the later passages.

The first major poem of Pushkin I loved was *The Gypsies*, written while Pushkin was in exile in Southern Russia. He had seen at first hand the nomadic gypsies on the Bessarabian steppes, and knew the encampments he describes. As so often in his verse, it is the character of the central woman Zemfira who is drawn with most energy, and whose taunting independence prefigures Bizet's Carmen. Two very different poets tackled passages from this poem. I have included a substantial extract from John Fuller's complete translation which is entirely at ease with the technical problems in finding natural rhyme, and a tone of voice close to Pushkin in period. Jo Shapcott, in contrast, has been inspired to produce a late twentieth-century version of some passages which she has made entirely her own, using Pushkin more as inspiration than text.

So many different voices blend together to suggest a man of many faces. This seems entirely appropriate for a poet who was in any case an intriguing and paradoxical figure. Pushkin was the child of a feckless Russian aristocrat and a descendant of the African slave who became a favourite of Peter the Great. He lived under an autocracy more tyrannical than any in Europe and his youthful poems in praise of personal freedom led to his exile in the South by the Tsar Alexander I. He was never admitted into the Decembrist plot against the new Tsar Nicholas, however, even though some of the conspirators were his closest friends, and his poems were found among the papers of all the leading figures. No one could have doubted Pushkin's courage; he was a cool duellist and eager for adventure. His close friends knew his genius, admired his wit, but perhaps doubted his commonsense. Indeed, it is part of Pushkin's isolation that few of them realised how much his intelligence had matured in the long years since his exile at the age of twenty-one.

Pushkin had affairs with some of the most beautiful women of his time—and once wrote a Don Juan list of their first names into the album of a young girl—yet he always believed himself ugly, perhaps because his mother mocked him so cruelly in his childhood. He was proud of his African great-grandfather Gannibal, but when writing a fictional account of Gannibal's sexual experience in a white world, Pushkin caricatured his ancestor's face as almost simian in his working notebooks. In spite of thinking himself equally unattractive, he chose for his wife the beautiful seventeen-year-old Natalya Goncharova, some thirteen years younger than himself, who loved balls and clothes and took little interest in literature. In time Natalya attracted the attentions of a handsome French officer, Baron d'Anthès, and at thirty-seven, Pushkin was killed in a duel fought to defend her honour.

The enthusiasm of Marina Tsvetaeva and Anna Akhmatova led me to my own vision of Pushkin. Tsvetaeva portrays the poet as quintessentially an outsider. She remembered how, when she visited the Pushkin monument in Moscow as a child, the *blackness* of the stone seemed a revelation: 'A black giant among white children . . . The Russian poet—is a *Negro*.' All Russian poets, she insisted, were visibly different from, and inevitably cast out or struck down by, the conformist multitude.

In this bicentenary year of his birth, it is time for Pushkin to take his rightful place on the world stage: as triumphant an example of poetry victorious over this world's celebrities as you will find. Anna Akhmatova has expressed that triumph most memorably. 'All the beauties, ladies in waiting, mistresses to the salons, Dames of the Order of St Catherine, members of the Imperial court, ministers, aides-de-camp, gradually began to be referred to as "contemporaries of Pushkin", and at length have been simply laid to rest (with their dates of birth and death garbled) in the indexes to editions of Pushkin's works.'

ELAINE FEINSTEIN
February 1999

CAROL ANN DUFFY

Poet to Prose-writer

Leave it to me, prose-writer.
You need a nose-wiper, someone
who shoots from the lip,
Give me a line—
I'll sharpen its tip,
weather it, feather it with rhyme,
send it flying
over enemy lines.
Prose is a pea-shooter, slow, narrow.
Poetry's an outlaw's bow-and-arrow.

'I loved you once'

I loved you once. If love is fire, then embers
smoulder in the ashes of this heart.
Don't be afraid. Don't worry. Don't remember.
I do not want you sad now we're apart.

I loved you without language, without hope,
now mad with jealousy, now insecure.
I loved you once so purely, so completely,
I know who loves you next can't love you more.

Style

Grace in anything eludes you.
Style and you are worlds apart.
When you're clever, thought deludes you.
When you're beautiful, you fart.

Echo

The end of silence. Thunder's peal.
Rain's well-thumbed pearls. A wildcat's snarl.
The singing childhood of a girl . . .
All these you hear
and send your voice back on the empty air,
then disappear.

You listen to the sigh of surf,
the shepherd's lonely shout, sheep's cough,
the grumbling clouds. Your own voice, soft,
but always clear,
replies, a poet's, living,
in the ear.

Ravenous

Two ravens fly.
One raven's cry
caws for dinner.
Otherwise, thinner

ravens in the sky.
Then one raven's eye
spies beneath a willow
a murdered fellow,

killed by whom? How? Why?
His falcon saw him die.
His hearse-black mare
and his mistress were there.

But the falcon flies high.
The horse rides by.
The girl waits for her lover
to arrive, alive, another.

Thou and You

By a slip of her sweet tongue
hard *you* was not spoken,
but soft *thou* sung
and my heart, used, broken,
was whole again, young.

I heard my own stiff voice
thank her politely:
how nice of *you*.
Why make that choice
when I thought how I love *thee*?

EAVAN BOLAND

Winter Road

Mist shifts and turns.
The moon breaks through it.
Gloomy clearings fill with
gloomy moonlight.

A winter road. Grim swish and rush
of a troika covering the miles.
Over and over: the echo and answer
of a sleigh bell.

I suppose you could find yourself
here and there in my driver's singing—
here high spirits—
and there longing.

No hut ahead. No light.
Just snow and loneliness.
Nothing to meet me on this road
but—one by one—these striped milestones.

How drab it is! But tomorrow I will be back
with Nina. Back to love. Back to better times—
my eyes unwilling to stop gazing
even when I nod off by the flames.

And when the hour hand closes
its circle beside us,
so be it. For once this midnight
will not divide us.

But Nina, if you only knew—how wretched this is!
The sleigh bell is ringing.
The moon is clouded over. Even my driver
is half-asleep. He has stopped singing.

Echo

After the sound of an animal howling.
After the thunder. After the horn.
After the song of a mountain woman
There is silence and empty air.
Then you are there.

You listen. The thunder calls.
You listen. The waves are speaking.
You answer. But no one will ever
Answer you. And you know it.
And the same is true for you

—poet!

BILL MANHIRE

Inesilla

I am here, Inesilla,
gazing up at your window.
All of Seville
is darkness and sleep.

I am here with my cloak,
with my guitar and sword,
with what makes me bold.
I am here at your window.

Do you sleep, Inesilla? Well
I will soon wake you with song,
and if the old fellow stirs
there's always this blade.

Ah let fall from the sill
that handhold of silk.
Why are you so slow?
Can it mean there's a rival?

I am here, Inesilla.
I am here at your window.
All of Seville
is darkness and sleep.

The Album

What can you gain from my name?
It will die—like the sad scrawl
of a wave on a far-off shore,
like night as it sighs in the woods.

On the pale, remembering page
there'll be only a trace,
marks on a headstone
in some strange, untranslatable tongue.

For what can remain? Lost
in the years and the tempests of feeling,
my name cannot last in your life
like some delicate keepsake.

Yet on a day of despair, in a small space
of calm, say it out of your sadness; say
'Somewhere I may still be remembered;
there's a heart in the world, where I live.'

TED HUGHES

The Prophet

Crazed by my soul's thirst
Through a dark land I staggered.
And a six-winged seraph
Halted me at a crossroads.
With fingers of dream
He touched my eye-pupils.
My eyes, prophetic, recoiled
Like a startled eaglet's.
He touched my ears
And a thunderous clangour filled them,
The shudderings of heaven,
The huge wingbeat of angels,
The submarine migration of sea-reptiles
And the burgeoning of the earth's vine.
He forced my mouth wide,
Plucked out my own cunning
Garrulous evil tongue,
And with bloody fingers
Between my frozen lips
Inserted the fork of a wise serpent.
He split my chest with a blade,
Wrenched my heart from its hiding,
And into the open wound
Pressed a flaming coal.
I lay on stones like a corpse.
There God's voice came to me:
'Stand, Prophet, you are my will.
Be my witness. Go
Through all seas and lands. With the Word
Burn the hearts of the people.'

(*From an annotated literal translation by Daniel Weissbort*)

CHRISTOPHER REID

Away From it All

Lucky you, if you can keep out of the fray
    And beyond the reach of dopes,
Dividing your energies between work and play,
    Memories and hopes;
Blest by Fate, surrounded by friends alone
    And protected, thank God,
From both the nincompoop's soporific drone
    And the shakings-awake of the clod.

To a Foreign Girl

In a language you can't read
   I rhyme farewell,
Kidding myself that with this screed
   I'll cast a spell.

Sweetest, until I fall apart
   And fade from the scene,
You—and you alone, sweetheart—
   Shall be my queen.

Eyes fixed on other men, may you
   Subscribe to my
Great passion, as you used to do
   Without knowing why.

Unmistakable

Not long ago, I dashed off some verses
And had them printed without my name.
Some bastard reviewer covered them with curses—
Anonymously, just the same!

We'd both crossed one of nature's laws:
Such sly manoeuvres never pay.
He'd known me at once by my terrible claws,
While it was his ears gave him away.

'The season's last flowers yield'

The season's last flowers yield
More than those first in the field.
The thoughts they rouse, sharp, sweet,
Have an incomparable power.
Likewise, the parting hour
As against when we merely meet.

'When I gather your slenderness'

When I gather your slenderness
    Into my embrace
And words of tenderness
    Pour out apace,

In answer, you unhook
    Your lissom form
And shoot me an old-fashioned look
    That is far from warm;

Then deep in your mind
    You sort out stuff
About men who have been unkind,
    While I huff and I puff . . .

Oh, a thousand damnations
    On my youthful appetite
For garden assignations
    In the dead of night,

On whispered imbecilities,
    On poetic pretence,
On girls' susceptibilities
    And their echoing laments!

'She gives you such looks'

She gives you such looks,
Such animated babble,
Such *jeux d'esprit*, such jokes,
Such expressions of delight,
And only last night
Beneath the dinner-table
I felt her little foot . . .

RANJIT BOLT

Tsar Nikita and His Daughters

There once lived, in a bygone day
An emperor, idle, rich and gay;
Tsar Nikita was his name
And all he touched he left the same,
So scant was the effect he had,
He did no good, he did no bad,
Neither created nor destroyed
But in his reign the realm enjoyed
Unparalleled prosperity.
While, as for Tsar Nikita, he
Dealt now and then with state affairs
And ate, and drank, and said his prayers,
And fathered forty daughters too
On sundry women—daughters who
Were angels all, vivacious, sweet,
With raven hair and dainty feet,
Perfect in every outward part,
Noble in spirit, and in heart,
Adorable from head to foot,
And *in* their pretty heads, to boot
Were minds to make you lose *your* mind,
You'd have to scour the world to find
Such specimens of womanhood,
Or charms less easily withstood . . .
One thing was missing . . . 'Is that all?'
I hear you cry. 'Twas, oh, so small—
Scarcely a problem—nonetheless,
For all its negligibleness,
It *was* still missing . . . how the Hell
Am I explicitly to tell
My readers what this one thing was?
I'm not sure if I can because
That pompous, pious, pea-brained dunce
The censor would explode at once . . .
Between their legs—oh, dear dear dear!
No, even that is far too clear—

32

Much too indecent—let me see,
A little more obliquity—
Let's find a more circuitous route
To lead you deftly, gently to't—
All right then: I of course adore
Venus's breasts, I love still more
Her luscious lips and little feet,
But those attractions can't compete
With . . . let's just say they're not the goal
Of my desire, which is a—hem!
A tiny thing, *nothing*, in fact—
Well that's what these princesses lacked,
Poor, sweet, vivacious girls. This gap,
This physiological mishap,
Caused consternation in the court,
Rendered their poor papa distraught,
Drew from their mothers tears and curses.
When word was let out by their nurses
The courtiers gaped and ahed and oohed,
Some were astonished, others rude,
While most made do with wide-eyed wonder
The rude ones laughed at nature's blunder,
Though only up their sleeves, of course,
Fearing Siberia, or worse.
Nikita summoned the distraught
Nurses and mothers, and the court
Before his royal presence and
Pronounced the following command:
'If any here should ever dare
To make my poor dear girls aware
Of what it is they haven't got
Or mention . . . mention God knows what
Or drop a hint or wink an eye
Or stick a finger up, then I—
And mark me well, I promise you
I jest not now, I seldom do—
It's not a thing to jest *about*—
Will either have their tongues cut out
If they are women, or if men . . .
I dread to think what I'll do then—
An organ worse than tongues will go—

An adjunct that can shrink and grow!'
Such was his potent interdict,
As right and just as it was strict,
As eloquent as it was clear,
And they all bowed their heads in fear,
Each listened well and took it in,
Resolving to preserve their skin,
Keep mum no matter what it cost
Lest something dearer should be lost.
The wives were most concerned about
Their husbands blurting something out,
While husbands, weary of their wives,
Now glimpsed the chance of quieter lives—
'If only she would blab!' they thought.
What grief they caused throughout the court,
Those poor princesses, as they grew,
And what compassionate tears they drew
From every eye! The sad affair
Was soon brought up in council, where
Nikita, whispering for fear
That some stray menial might hear,
Quickly, succinctly, sought ideas
From the assembled senior peers.
They fell to wondering: was there not
Some remedy, and if so what?
At length an ancient fellow rose—
He scratched his head and tapped his nose
Bowed to them all and thus began:
'Wise sovereign, pardon an old man
If he appear impertinent,
My words, if coarse, are kindly meant . . .
Well then, here goes: I used to know
A *bawd*, a long long time ago,
I don't know what she's doing now,
Perhaps still pimping—anyhow
People believed she was a witch
For there was not one ailment which
She couldn't cure—beyond a doubt
That woman's well worth seeking out.
She'll find a cure, if there is one,
Insert . . . well, do what must be done.'

'Then someone fetch her! Track her down!'
The Tsar cried, and an angry frown
Darkened his brow. 'But should she try
To trick or trap us, or to lie,
And fail to give us what we want,
Call me a rogue, a miscreant
If I don't have her burned—I swear
As God's my witness!'
                                    Everywhere
The witch was looked for, far and wide
Went secret messengers supplied
With mounts as fast as any, and
With passports good throughout the land.
Off they all scampered, near and far
Seeking the witch out for the Tsar.
A year went by, a second flew
And blanks were all the envoys drew,
Until one zealous messenger
At long, long last caught up with her
In a dark forest (I dare say
The Devil had pointed him that way),
A wood he'd ridden into, where
He found a cote, and living there
Who but the ancient sorceress.
Being the Tsar's envoy, no less,
Dispensing with formalities
He went in boldly as you please
And told her of his sovereign's plight—
How the princesses weren't quite right
In one respect. Immediately
The old witch grasped what that must be.
'Be off with you at once!' she said
'And don't look back or else you're dead!
You'll catch a fever! But return
In three days' time and then you'll learn
What I prescribe; I'll have for you
A package to deliver. Shoo!
Dawn on the fourth day—not before.'
With that she pushed him out the door.
The old witch locked herself away
With coal to last till the fourth day,

And for the next three nights and days
Conjured the Devil in sundry ways
Being versed in every single spell
That ever drew him out of Hell.
At length he came to her, and brought
A box containing every sort
Of what we sinful men adore,
Yes, every taste was catered for,
Every shape and size was there,
Each with its tufts of curly hair.
Each one her expert eye assessed,
She then picked out the forty best,
Wrapped them in a napkin and
Stowed them in Satan's box. As planned
The envoy was dispatched with these
And with a rouble, if you please,
A silver rouble for the road.
He took them and away he rode.
He galloped on till day was done
And, when he saw the setting sun,
Resolved to eat and quench his thirst
Before he went another verst.
He was an adept of the road
And in his travel bag had stowed
Food, vodka, cutlery—had thought
Of all necessities, in short,
So now he tethered up his horse
And started on the opening course.
His horse grazed quietly, while he
Day-dreamed of new prosperity,
Promotion from the Tsar, to count
Or prince. As expectations mount
A question forms in his dull brain:
'What might the magic box contain?
What has the old witch sent the Tsar?
Oh, what a nuisance padlocks are!'
The need to know may drive him mad
His curiosity's that bad;
He lays an agitated ear
Against the lid but cannot hear
The slightest sound, though he can smell

An odour he knows all too well.
'What's in this box? I have to know!
There's no alternative!' And so
The silly fellow took his life
Into his hands, and with a knife
Prised the box open . . . as he did,
As soon as he'd removed the lid,
The forty . . . improprieties
Flew out and perched up in the trees
Flashing their tails like mating fowl.
The messenger let out a howl
Then called to them, until his head
Was throbbing, tried with bits of bread
And crumbs to lure them down, in vain.
'They don't eat bread, that much is plain,'
He thinks. They chirrup in the trees,
Enjoy themselves and take their ease,
The box is not their cup of tea
They'd rather perch up in a tree.
Then up there plods along the road
An ancient crone all bent and bowed
With age, and leaning on a stick.
The messenger, by now frantic,
Fell at the beldame's feet and said:
'Please help me or I'll lose my head!
Please, mother! Look what's happened here!
They won't come back! I'm sick with fear!'
The hag looked up and hissed and spat.
'You ninny, carrying on like that!
It serves you right! Still, don't you fret,
Show them your whatsit, quick, my pet,
They'll all come down when they see that
And sharpish, or I'll eat my hat!'
No sooner was the whatsit shown
Than all the thingummies flew down.
They settled in their box once more
And promptly making it secure
He headed home without delay.
The forty things were stowed away
Where they belonged—that is to say
Between Nikita's daughters' legs.

37

To celebrate their new-found sex
Their father held a sumptuous feast.
A week-long banquet; all work ceased
For one whole month; rewards there were
Not only for the messenger
But all the councillors as well—
That's almost all there is to tell—
The witch was not forgotten either,
Two poisonous snakes preserved in ether
From the museum, handsome ones,
Also two lovely skeletons
Were her reward. And that's the end.
Now carp at me. I don't intend
To justify this tale to you.
Why tell it? Well, I wanted to!

ALLEN CURNOW

The Upas Tree

Scorched unforgiving soil
burned off burned out
in summer conflagrations

half-way to the horizon
look for the Upas Tree
no other created thing
to be seen than this

grim guard

                the parched
steppes convulsed
at its birth
and a deathly day that was
loading root and branch with
instant poison
visibly in the heat of noon
sweated out by nightfall
globuled and beaded
thick thick
              and clear
the concentrate
lethal
         the small birds
drop dead from the sky
outside the dripline of its leaves
the tiger
gives it a wide berth

only the black whirlwind
swarms up it and out again
with death to deliver
and any passing cloud
sprinkling its foliage
carries across the hot sand

its poisonous rain

'Find that tree
Bring back the deadly stuff'
his imperial master said
and off he went
and by morning brought
one resinous lump
and one withering branch
and fell to the rush-strewn floor
of the great tent
to die at the feet
of his Lord now possessed of
invincible power

and that power made
him such murderous missiles
as devastated
neighbouring realms
and subjected
them and their peoples
by life's death-dealing arts.

When and Where

Where the big crowds come, the street,
the stadium, the park where the young
go crazy to the beat
and the heated bubble of the song,

thoughts running loose, I tell
myself, the years will have blipped past,
one by one the lot of us here present will
be gone into the dark. Someone's last

hour's always next, right here and now.
Deep under the bark of that great oak
my father's lifetime's told in rings, which grow
to outlive me too. Gently as I stroke

this child's head, I'm thinking, 'Goodbye!
It's all yours now, the season's crop—
your time to bud, and bloom, while my
late leaves wither and drop—

And which day of which year
to come will turn out to have been
the anniversary, distant or near,
of my death? Good question. The scene,

will it be wartime, on a trip,
or at home or in some nearby
street, crashed coach or a ship-
wreck that I'm to die?

Cadavers couldn't care less where they rot,
yet the living tissue leans (as best it may)
toward the long-loved familiar spot
for its rest. Mine does, think of it that way.

Freshly dug. Young things, chase your ball.
Nature's not watching, only minding
by its own light perpetual
beauty of its own fact or finding.

The Talisman

A warmer latitude.
An unvisited
beach.
      Rocks wetted where
the last wave broke.
          Some
such night as this lit
by a swollen moon's
foggy glow.
        Somewhere
the Pasha (of these parts)
relaxing sucks at the
narghile the sweet
fume inhaling.
         Was it
there this ravishingly
wise woman whose hands caressed
me pressed something small
into mine?
      Keep it.
It's a talisman.
Keep it safe. It's got
powers that love gave.
         Listen
while I tell you all
you need to know about
this precious thing.
        Sick
it won't cure you. No
earthly use either in
the hour of death or day
of disaster.
      Nor will it
win you the Lottery
crown you superstar
jet you happily home
(soured expatriate!) No.

But when cheating eyes
meet and you're aroused
oh my darling! (she said)
and lips after dark
unlovingly kiss
                  That's
when it kicks in – this
talisman of mine
                  you'll
never be two-timed
left for dead bleeding
newly from the heart!

CHARLES TOMLINSON

Grapes

I shall not regret the roses,
Fading when the spring has gone;
I like the grapes, too, on their vine
In clusters ripe with hillside sun,
The glory of my fertile valley,
Gold autumn's bliss where tendrils curl
With grapes as oblong and translucent
As the fingers of a girl.

To the Sea

Farewell, free element!
For the last time before me
You roll the blueness of your waves
And gleam in pride of beauty.

Like the last words of a friend,
His murmurs of departure,
Your doleful sound, your sound of summons
Are valedictions to the ear.

Native region of my soul,
How often following your coast
In silence, shut in contemplation,
I've sought the intent I feared was lost.

How your call-notes called to me,
Muffled roarings, voice of the abyss,
Wilful groundswell of your surge
And your evening silences.

By mere caprice you choose to spare
The humble sail of fishermen
That rides the breakers without fear,
A playful mood waylays you where
A whole fleet founders then.

I did not make myself forgo
The dull immobile shore,
To greet you with a burst and glow
And let your heaving wave-crests show
The true shape of poetic rapture.

You waited, called. I was enchained;
My spirit could not struggle free,
But by the waters' edge remained
Spellbound by such fervency.

What is there to regret? Where now
Would I direct my carefree way?

One object in your wilderness
Might have seized upon my fancy.

One cliff, sepulchre of glory . . .
There the memories of fame
Submitted to the chill of sleep,
Extinguished with Napoleon's flame.

There rest came to him. In his wake
Another genius guttered out
Amid the roar of tempest—
Byron, that potentate of thought.

He vanished, mourned by Liberty,
Leaving the world his wreath and soul;
Roar out, rear up, you storm-tossed sea:
He bade your waves to roll.

He was created out of you:
Your image left on him its mark,
Like you undaunted by what passed,
Like you a presence deep and dark.

The world has emptied. Where now, sea,
Will you bear me on my way?
Earth's lot is wide monotony.
A drop of bliss? Looms already
Enlightenment or tyrant's sway.

Farewell, sea—I shall not forget
How your festive beauty shone,
My ear will never lose that sound,
That deep roar as the dark comes on.

To the silence of the forest,
Still full of you beneath the leaves,
I shall take the bays and cliffs,
Shade, glitter, murmur of the waves.

Winter Road

Across the wavering hazes
Moon is breaking on the sight,
Across each melancholy clearing
Pours a melancholy light.

Down the wintry dismal road
Runs the troika, and the tone
Of its tuneless sleigh-bell
Monotonously jangles on . . .

One hears the old familiar note
In the coachman's lengthy song,
Drunk carousal yielding place
To lament and lover's wrong . . .

Not a light, no darkened cabin,
Silence, snow. As I pass by
Only mileposts with their ciphers
Attend me on my endless way.

Dismal, dreary . . . but tomorrow,
Nina, returning to you there,
I shall never gaze my fill
Dreaming and gazing by the fire.

Tunefully the circling clock
Will complete its measured round,
And removing the intruders
For us that midnight will not sound.

Dismal, Nina, drear my journey,
Quiet the coachman—sleep has won;
Monotonous the sleigh-bell's jangle,
Cloud has blotted back the moon.

DANNIE ABSE

Tempest

When lightning flashes and the night ignites
look out for the girl on the high cliff.
See how magically she's dressed in white;
how the enormous sea pitches and flings
its lascivious spray towards her;
how the brash outrageous wind struggles, clings
to her raiments as if to unrobe her.
Heaven's royal blue has been deleted
but majestical those swirling clouds
and the sea rising up to fall and crash;
yet more majestic still that maid in white
briefly visible in the lightning flash.

A Little Bird

In this alien land I must cling
to native tradition, release
one bird from cramped captivity,
this radiant holiday of Spring.

In doing so I cease to rage
against God. I have no need to
as long as I am free to set free
one trembling creature from its cage.

'As the drooping autumn flowers'

As the drooping autumn flowers touch us
more plangently than those that blaze in Spring
so the pigeon mood returns of when we parted
more than those candied minutes when we courted
and timelessness was everything.

The Emperor Nicholas I

Working wonders
100 per cent alive
our new Tsar
(hurrah)
immediately sent
120 to Siberia.
Hung 5.

To Dawe, Esq.*

Why let your magic pencil insist
my Moorish profile survive the ages?
Heinous Mephistopheles himself would arch
his back and hiss at it. Sir, desist.

Draw instead lovely Olenina.
To your own genius be dutiful.
In blaze of inspiration pay homage
only to youth and to the beautiful.

---

* George Dawe (1781–1829). English portrait painter and mezzotint engraver in the manner of Sir Joshua Reynolds. Went to Russia and was named First Painter to the Court of Russia by Alexander I who had him paint about four hundred portraits of army men who served in the Napoleonic Wars. Several of Dawe's paintings hang in the Hermitage Museum in St Petersburg.

To A. A. Davydova*

My Aglaya, you could not resist this one
—his uniform, his black curly moustache;
or that one—so attractively stashed with cash.
And he who need only whisper in French to score.
Also Cleon—such conversational skill;
and Damis whose throaty singing could thrill
you to pieces. But tell me, my dear,
What did your husband wed *you* for?

I know how you were always bowled over
by sportsmen and swordsmen. So you were had,
my dear, by that kilted somersaulting peer
(easy to adore) and by those Englishmen
you called Sir Lancelot and Galahad
(though both, I think, a little queer).
Well, there are 365 knights in a year.
What did you wed your husband for?

* Aglaya Davydova, née Duchesse de Grammont, the promiscuous wife of General Alexander Davydov (the southern Decembrist's brother), whose favours Pushkin also enjoyed briefly.

ELAINE FEINSTEIN

Aglaya

One man I know had my Aglaya
For his moustache and uniform.
Money won her for another.
Any Frenchman roused her warmth.
Cleon's mind excited her,
And Damis with his tender song.
Tell me, though, my dear Aglaya,
How did your spouse win your desire?

CHARLES TOMLINSON

The Bronze Horseman

INTRODUCTION

Desolate flowed the waters: he
standing upon their shore and full
with the prospect of his thoughts
gazed distance down: the pull
of the river's sweep and breadth
fronted him here: a dug-out skiff
sped by in vistaed loneliness:
the shores of moss and swamp let show
black huts in which the wretched Finn
huddles himself against the snow:
and forest which the light of sun
shut-back by mist had never known
soughed round: his thoughts thrust on:
From here our threat shall reach the Swede
and here a city shall arise
to spite our neighbour's haughtiness:
for we by Nature are decreed
to hack out through the wooden wall
a window upon Europe and
firm-footed stand beside the sea:
on waves to them unknown till now
all the flags shall be our guests
and we shall feast them all.

Lapse of a century and then
the young metropolis, the harsh
north's ornament and wonder
from forest darkness, swamp of marsh
rose up in its pride and splendour:
where, in other times the Finn,
woeful stepson there of Nature's,
cast worn nets to unknown waters,
space now feels the living touch
and crowds and kindles with the grace

and bulk of palaces and towers.
Speeding from all the ends of earth
ships thicken at each loaded wharf:
Neva has clad herself in granite:
across those waters bridges span:
and now the islands wear the green
luxury of garden shade:
before the younger capital
our ancient Moscow now—
a widow in imperial purple—
before a new-crowned queen must fade.

Peter's creation, I admire
your scapes both graceful and severe,
the Neva's sovereign flow,
cast-iron rail and granite shapes
along the banks, the nights which grow
pensive in that transparent dusk,
that moonless brilliance when I
within my room can write and read
needing no lamp, and clear out there
sleep crowding, desolate streets, and bright
glints the Admiralty spire:
refusing to the dark its right
to trespass on the golden height,
the glow that's hurrying to replace
the glow that's gone will grant no more
to night itself than one half hour.
I love, once cruel winter's here,
the frost and the unyielding air,
sledges that take the river-course,
more vivid than the rose the cheeks
of girls, and all the glancing brightness,
the noise and talk of dancing,
the glasses seething to the brim,
over the punch the flames' blue play
while young men drink the night away:
I love the animation,
the show of war as, square on square,
infantry and horses fill
the Fields of Mars, and teach the eye

a beauty in monotony:
the order and the undulation
of threadbare flags that won their day,
the glitter of the brazen casques
that, bullet-holed, survived the fray.

Military capital,
I love your fortress' smoke and thunder
when the Tsarina of the north
gives the imperial house a son,
or the whole country celebrates
a victory new-won:
or breaking up its dark-blue ice
the Neva bears it to the seas
and, sensing spring, leaps on.

Display your beauty, city, stand
steadfast like our native land,
and may the conquered element
accept a mutual content:
let the Finnish waves put by
their ancient bonds, their enmity,
nor vainly, rancorously break
Peter's everlasting sleep.

There was a time—its shape still clear
within men's minds: a time of fear:
reader, I retell it now
and my tale's a tale of woe.

CAROL RUMENS

The Bronze Horseman

PART II

The raid was done. Neva recoiled.
She'd rampaged like a gang of hoods,
Revved the getaway car, and left
A trail of trashed, pathetic goods,
And hopeless wails of rape and theft.
Yevgeny watched as pavements surfaced
Muddily, took his chance, and raced
Down to the river. Still she boiled,
Lively as Mother Russia's kettle,
Foaming like horses after battle.

He paced the quay, almost despaired,
But clearer skies at last lured out
A ferryman, up for any job.
He had a crew, a sturdy boat.
Yevgeny shouted, waved a bob,
'You're on. Let's go!' Somehow they steered
A passage through the interlocked
Rabbles of wind and tide. They docked
At last, Yevgeny disappeared.

He dared not pause to see what reeled
Past as he ran, a killing-field:
The sea had raged against the Tsar
But merely proven her contempt
For clerks' small dreams of betterment.
The street curved to the bay not far
From where the house (please, God) would stand.
Here was the willow, yes, a paling
Torn from the fence. Yevgeny turned
Dizzily, his last hope failing.
There was no house. All it had held,
Brave beams and cosy beds, the best
China, the well-stocked sewing-kit,

And oh, the face, voice, heart of it
—Parasha—darling of his world—
Were nowhere. Swept away. He cursed,
Punched his brow and laughed the worst
Laugh on this earth.

                He couldn't rest
That night and neither could the shivering
City. Crowds, unhoused, unfed,
Lit candles, prayed the lost were living,
Counted the cost, counted the dead.
Dawn broke, peculiarly bright,
And people set to work. The shite
And mud were cleared, the bolted doors
Heaved open, and the ancient laws
By which cool tradesmen charge us double
So as to mitigate their trouble,
Rapidly resumed. Fine speeches
Rolled their purple. Red tape knotted
Where ministerial faults were spotted.
Boats were hauled back to the beaches.

Yevgeny tramped the city. Where
Was home but in his own despair?
The landlord gave him one week's grace
And then re-let the squalid space
To an impoverished poet, biting
The bullet of *Creative Writing*.

Yevgeny walked. Walked rain, walked gales,
Walked on the flood-beast's shimmering scales,
And fought it down and saw it still
Lash at Parasha's windowsill
And fold her in its jaws. He cried
To brass-badged stone for guns or ships
To rescue her, he kissed his bride,
Her willow hair, her muddy lips.
The only word his mutterings knew
Was hers—*Parasha*. Then that too
Slipped beyond his mental range.
A cardboard classroom by the wharf

Taught him the ropes. He learnt enough
To snatch a loaf. To beg spare change.

One night the river seemed to howl,
And beat her fists on pitiless stone:
Nightwatchmen bellowed through the gale.
Yevgeny wakened with a groan,
Got up and walked the streets. At last,
His jumbled thoughts ran clear. He knew
This square. He stopped. Rich moonlight glossed
The marble lion he'd clung to when
The flood grew taller than a man.
This was its playground, and its true
Source. And vividly he saw
Beyond the grandly-lifted paw,
The rearing horse and mounted Tsar
Peter, fused in brutal power,
One arm flung wide to signify
'This is my creation. I
Am master.' Something floodlike welled
Huge in Yevgeny's throat. He yelled
'Fuck your bastard creation. See
The mess you've made. Watch out for me!'

The bronze eyes and the human blaze
Together, then the pale one sways,
Turns and runs into the black
Shadows, screaming. At his back
The bronze hooves clatter. Poor Yevgeny,
Run, run with your kind—the many
Any Tsar can always spare . . .
Now, when he wanders past that square,
A strange delusion seems to sap
Yevgeny's strength. He doffs his cap
Awkwardly, and, scared to stay
A moment longer, limps away.

EDWIN MORGAN

'Winter in the country!'

Winter in the country! What to do? I see
My man coming in with my morning cup of tea,
Bombard him with questions: is it warm outside?
Less stormy? New snow? Could we go for a ride,
Leave bed for saddle? Or enjoy homelier scenes,
Lazing till dinner with my neighbour's old magazines?
It's powdery snow. Up and on horseback and away,
Trotting through the grass in the first light of day,
We clutch our whips and hear our dogs behind us;
We strain our eyes; pale snow is all around us;
We circle, sniff, and scour; by dusk we're empty men:
We've missed two hares, that's all; so home we go again.
Evening should be good: wild outside: the house shakes!
But the candle burns dim; my heart nips and aches,
I drink my deadly boredom drop by trickling drop.
Can I read? My eyes crawl down the lines and stop,
My thoughts are miles away . . . I close the book, I sit,
I take my pen, I strike my shrinking muse with it
And force out a few frowsty formless words.
But sound will not meet sound . . . I am left with mere shards
Of rhyme, my wayward handmaid's not on call:
The verse comes creeping cold and loath and slow and dull.
I'm tired of this fruitless wrestling with inspiration,
I go through to the parlour and listen to conversation
About the sugar factory, about the forthcoming election;
The hostess frowns, the weather matches her complexion,
Her steely knitting-needles flash and cross, unless
Her king of hearts unfolds a fortune-teller's guess.
Boredom! Day after day cut off from everything!
But if, in this dreary village, there should come an evening
When I am bent over a draughtboard in that room
And some distant carriage or sleigh should burst through the gloom
With its unexpected freight, an old woman, two girls
(Two friends, two strapping sisters shaking their blond curls)—
How they galvanise a place so dead and grim!
How life seems suddenly, dear God, full to the brim!

At first some carefully-careless sidelong glances pass,
Then comes a word or two, then talking lad-and-lass,
Then laughter as among friends, and 'just a song at twilight',
And whispering at table, and waltzes in full flight,
And O those melting looks, that cunning repartee,
Stolen moments under stairs for none to see!
One girl walks out onto the dark porch, alone,
Neck bare, breast bare, with her hair blizzard-blown!
But northern storms cannot beat down the Russian rose.
How hot a kiss can be that's snatched among the snows!
How fresh the Russian girl among the drifts and flakes!

Goofy and Daffy

OR THE TALE OF THE PRIEST
AND HIS HANDYMAN

Once upon a time, once upon a time,
Goofy the priest lived in this clime.
Goofy's off to the market
To fill his empty basket.
Who does he meet there
But Daffy, wandering spare.
'What got you up so early, father?
What odds and ends are you out to gather?'
'Not odds and ends, but a handyman:
Join wood, groom horses, put eggs in the pan.
Where can I find such
A servant, who mustn't cost much?'
Says Daffy: 'I'll serve you splendidly,
Diligently and wholeheartedly;
Give me regular boiled wheat for a year
And then I'll give you three clips on the ear.'
Goofy thinks and thinks,
Scratches his head, goes to the brink.
A crack on the pate is a crack on the pate,
But it might not happen (that's Russian for fate).
Says he to Daffy: 'All right!
Both of us will sleep at night.
Settle in at my house.
Prove your zeal, prove your *nous*!'
Daffy is soon at home with the priest,
Sleeps on straw like a beast,
Eats enough for four
But works like seven or more,
Gets things dancing along before dawn,
Harnesses horse at furrow, ploughs on, on,
Lights the oven, buys, prepares for the pot,
Boils the egg and shells it—does the lot!
Goofy's wife can't speak too highly of him,
Goofy's daughter makes sheep's eyes at him,
Goofy's young son calls him daddy,
He boils his gruel and dandles the laddie.

But Goofy fails to share all this affection,
He feels no cuddly predilection,
He thinks about the day of reckoning,
Time races, and the hour is beckoning,
He neither eats nor drinks nor sleeps at night,
His head cracks in advance, out of pure fright.
At last he makes his wife a full confession:
'And so . . . and so . . . O it's a hopeless position!'
The woman's wits were shrewd
To nose out every turpitude.
She tells him: 'I have a plan
To get us out of this frying-pan:
Give Daffy some task he cannot possibly do,
Yet he must do it fully through and through.
This will take the edge off your head-cracking.
Daffy gets no pay, we send him packing.'
The priest began to perk up now
And look on Daffy with a clearer brow.
He calls out: 'Come here my friend,
My trusty Daffy, my handyman: attend!
There are some devils that are committed
To pay me rent; only by my death is it remitted;
Fine income, you'd think, but arrears
Have piled up for three years.
So eat up your wheat, find
These devils, get my rent—all of it, mind!'
Knowing how futile priest-baiting would be,
Daffy goes off to sit by the sea.
There he twists a rope, throws
The end out till it's wet as a hose.
A wizened devil crawls out from the waves:
'What's it with Daffy? Something he craves?'
—'I want this rope to pucker and squeeze the sea,
To squeeze and torture you and your damned progeny.'—
This puts the old devil in a black mood.
'What makes you huff and puff and act so crude?'
—'What do you think? You must pay your rent,
You never remember the day it should be sent!
But now it's time for me to have some fun,
And you, you dogs, will be totally undone.'—
'Dear Daffy, wait! Don't pucker and squeeze the sea!

You'll get your rent in full, instantly!
Just wait, I'll send you my grandson. Wait!'
Thinks Daffy: 'This fool's easy meat!'
The slip of a devil surfaced as directed,
Mewed like a hungry kitten, genuflected:
'Good-day, good man Daff, how much
Rent do we owe you, for such
Details were never told us,
Oh no, such anxieties never enfold us!
What the hell—take it, but with one condition:
It's our general verdict, and my mission
Is to tell you, to avoid future fuss:
We must race round the sea, and the one of us
Who wins, wins all the rent; look,
They're getting the bag ready off the hook.'
Daffy is crafty, laughs to himself:
'What a would-be satanic elf!
Think you could ever tangle with me,
With Daffy, this Daffy, could ever be
My adversary! There's me—and another:
Wait till you see my younger brother!'
Daffy runs to the nearest little wood,
Catches two hares, bags them tight and good,
Back then to the seashore,
To the sea-devils once more.
Daffy pulls one hare out by its ear:
'Dance now, it's my balalaika you hear;
And you, little devil, you're so young,
You're so feeble, I'm so strong,
What a contest, waste of time!
Outstrip my brother? Get in line.
One, two, three! Catch up if you can!'
So hare and devils ran and ran.
Devil followed the sea-shore,
Hare made for the woods once more.
What next then?—having rounded the sea,
With his snout in the air and his tongue lolling free,
Panting fit to burst, at the end of his run,
Pawing off the sweat, wet to the bone,
The devil thinks: Daffy's beaten, I've won!
But look: there's Daffy, stroking his own,

His brother, his hare: 'Sweet brother dear,
You're weary, poor thing, take a rest here.'
The demon, struck dumb,
Tail between legs, totally overcome,
Squints up at the brother-hare,
Says: 'Wait—I'll get the rent, it's there.'
Goes to his grandad, tells him: 'Bad trip!
Daffy the younger gave me the slip!'
The old devil starts to think dark thoughts,
But Daffy blows the sea into knots,
Roars the waves wide in a scatter.
The little demon appears with his patter:
'You'll have all your rent, squire, but see this stick:
Listen now: I want you to pick
A favoured target, and the one
Who throws farthest gets the rent. What fun!
You don't think so? Your wrist might break?
What are you waiting for?'—'For that cloud to make
A good target; then I'll hurl your stick there,
Cause a cloudburst; devils will go spare.'
—The demon quakes, runs to his grandad,
Daffy has won again, it's bad!
And Daffy roars over the sea once more
And threatens the rope: 'I'll make the devils sore!'
The demon pops out again: 'Shush, shush,
If you really want the rent, we're flush—'
—'Too late,' says Daffy, 'too late!
It is my turn to state
The terms, my little enemy, and ask
You to complete a little task.
Let's find out how strong you are.
See that grey mare?
Take up the mare, and bear
That mare for half a kilometre;
You carry her, the rent is yours:
If you miscarry, I win my arrears.'
The wretched little devil
Starts to hump and swivel
Under the mare, straining
Up there, spraining,
Ups the mare, takes two steps, falls

On the third, sprawls.
Says Daffy: 'Stupid demon, what
Made you think you could cut this knot?
Arms are useless, it's legs you need.
Watch me mount her like a steed.'
Daffy bestrides the mare without fuss,
Gallops his kilometre in a column of dust.
Nothing for it now—the devils bring back
Daffy's rent collected in a sack.
And Daffy starts quacking like a duck,
But Goofy, at the sight of him, runs amuck,
Hides behind his wife,
Shaking in fear of his life.
Daffy finds him, gives him the rent,
Demands the fee that can't be spent.
The poor priest's made
To lift his head:
At the first blow he's reeling
Up to the ceiling;
At the next blow he's dumb,
Quite lost his tongue;
At the third blow his mind
Is totally undermined.
Daffy has thumped a judgement not to be lost:
'Father, don't chase cheapness at any cost!'

JOHN FULLER

From THE GYPSIES

In Bessarabia a crew
Of raucous gypsies pitched their tent
At nightfall everywhere they went.
Any old river bank would do.
Their camp shone bright as liberty,
Tranquil their sleep beneath the moon;
On wagon wheels a canopy
Of hanging rugs was semi-strewn
Above the fire; round it they
Prepared their supper; horses where
They stood were grazing; and there lay,
Untethered near the tent, a bear.
The steppes were alive with people doing
Each little thing (when they review
The next day's trek) that they must do,
Women's songs and boys' hullooing,
Clang of the hammered iron shoe.
But soon on that nomadic band
Fell sleepy silence: nothing there
But stillness apprehended and
The whine of dog or whinny of mare.
And now they put out every light
And all was still; the lunar lamp,
Lonely from her heavenly height,
Shone luminous upon the camp.
One old man in his tent, awake,
Warm by his campfire, stooped to rake
Its embers and looked up to gaze
At distant fields where he could make
Out little, through the night's deep haze.
Constantly ready for a lark,
His daughter'd gone to take a turn
Upon the moors; she would return,
But here it was already dark,
Not long before the moon would set
Behind the scud of sky—the old

67

Man knew she often wandered, yet
His little supper still got cold.
      But here she was. Not on her own
But with a young man following
Who to the gypsy was unknown.
'Father,' said the girl. 'I bring
A visitor. I found him near
The hill out there. I knew that you
Would not object to his being here.
He wants to be a gypsy too.
His name's Aleko, and I'll be
His sweetheart willingly. Although
An outlaw, he will come with me
Wherever I may I choose to go.'

Old Man

      I'm glad. Till morning I consent
To have you with us in our tent
Or for a longer stay if you
Would like. We are of one accord
To share with you both bed and board.
Be one of us—be poor; be who
You are, free to do what you do—
And tomorrow at the earliest
We'll set off in that wagon there;
How do you want to spend your time?
Smithying? Singing songs? Well, I'm
Easy. Perhaps you'll lead the bear?

Aleko

      I'll stay!

Zemfira

            O then I shall be blest!
He will be mine! No one can keep
Him from me . . . now the new moon's crest
Has set; the pastures are possessed
By mist, and I myself by sleep.
                  *
      Dawn. And the old man quietly
Wandered round the silent tent.

'You must get up, Zemfira: see,
The sun is rising. Up, my friend!
My children, leave your bed of joy!'
Out came the gypsies, chattering;
The tents came down; the cart convoy
Was ready to get journeying.
Everything took off at once—
A crowd in haste upon the track;
Donkeys with baskets on their back
Full of excited children; throngs
Of women followed, wives and mothers,
Old men, young men, husbands, brothers;
Yelling, bustle, gypsy songs,
The roaring of the bear, the restless
Rattling of his chains, their togs
So brightly coloured and so shabby,
Old men naked as a baby,
The barks and yelping of the dogs,
Creak of the cart, the bagpipe's whine,
Higgledy-piggledy, crude, pathetic,
Yet always brisk and energetic,
So foreign to this life of mine,
Its idle deadly pleasures, long
And tedious as a galley-song!

Zemfira
    All these things that you forego,
Dear, do you miss them, do you care?

Aleko
    What sort of things are these?

Zemfira
                               You know:
    Your city life, the people there.

Aleko
    What is there I should miss? My dear,
You can't, you've simply no idea
Of the servility of towns!
Crowds of people penned in there

Like cattle, ignorant of the air
And scents of the spring downs;
Ashamed of love, hostile to thought,
To bondage they are eager debtors,
Their very worship may be bought:
They pray for riches and for fetters.
What have I foregone? The throb
Of the betrayed heart, prejudice,
The hurry of the heedless mob,
The ostentatiousness of vice.

Zemfira

But think of the assembly rooms,
The brilliant tapestries, the games,
The murmuring banquets, rare perfumes,
The ladies' gowns, the famous names—!

Aleko

Where is the joy in city whirls?
In the loveless city there's no joy.
You are much finer than the city girls
Though you've no necklaces, no pearls.
You are a jewel without alloy!
My love, please stay just as you are
And as for me I only plead
For love and idleness—to share
Your outcast life is all I need.

*

Two years went by. And still resigned
In quiet association those
Same gypsies wandered on to find
A ready welcome and repose.
Emancipated from the snare
Of culture, Aleko's abode
Was theirs; without a thought or care,
Like them he took the open road.
He and the family the same;
His previous life had little claim,
It was to the gypsy life he clung.
Lightheaded with their day-long ease,
He loved their camp beneath the trees

At night, their terse but sonorous tongue.
The steppes were all their settlement.
The bear, an exile from its lair,
Shaggy companion of his tent,
Near the Moldavian village where
The crowds came cautiously to look,
Danced lubberly and gnawed
The chain that chafed his nose, and roared;
Leaning on his traveller's crook,
The old man beat his tambourine,
Aleko sang and led the bear
About, Zemfira went between
Taking what villagers could spare.
Night fell; together all the three
Cooked their millet, took their fill;
The old man slept; tranquillity
Possessed the tent, all dark and still.

*

The old man's cooling blood the Spring
Quickened with sunshine from above;
His nursing daughter sang of love.
Aleko turned pale, listening.

Zemfira

Foul spouse, growly spouse,
Scar me or scald me.
I'm steady; I'm ready
For knife or for fire.

I abominate you,
You laughing-stock you,
There's another I love
To whom I am true.

Aleko

Be quiet. Stop this idiocy.
It's crude. Can't you sing something new?

Zemfira

So what? It's all the same to me!
Do you think I sing the song for you?

Scar me or scald me,
I'll never blab,
Foul spouse, growly spouse,
You'll not nab him.

Fresher than spring he is,
Hot as noon;
What youth, what stamina!
And I make him swoon!

In the still of the night
How I touched him there,
And oh how we sniggered
At your greying hair!

Aleko
  Silence, Zemfira! That's enough . . .

Zemfira
  So now you know my song is true?

Aleko
  Zemfira!

Zemfira
          No need to be so rough,
  But yes, I sing the song for you.

  (*Goes off singing 'Foul spouse', etc.*)
                    *
  A stilly night. A caravan
Of stars led by a silver sphere;
Zemfira quickly woke the old man:
'Father! Aleko scares me. Can
He still be sound asleep? I fear
These moans and whimpers. Can't you hear?'

Old Man
  Leave him alone. Don't say a word.
  A Russian legend that I've heard
  Explains how just at midnight we

72

May find a sleeper's breathing slurred
By a stifling sprite; but it will flee
At light of dawn. Come, sit with me.

Zemfira
Father! He's whispering 'Zemfira!'

Old Man
In sleep it's you he's thinking of:
Nothing in the world is dearer.

Zemfira
But I have fallen out of love.
I'm bored. I'd now like to be free
Already I . . . but hush! come near:
He breathes another's name. You see?

Old Man
Whose name?

Zemfira
                    A hoarse groan (you hear?)
And grinding of the teeth . . .! Why so?
I'll wake him up . . .

Old Man
                    You mustn't, no:
Do not drive out the midnight sprite,
It will depart . . .

Zemfira
                    He's turned, and spoken
To me, half-risen . . . now he's woken.
I'll go to him—sleep now, goodnight.

Aleko
Where have you been?

Zemfira
                    With Father. I
Thought that a spirit plagued you where

73

You slept, your soul in agony,
It seemed; you gave me such a scare!
You called me in your sleep and ground
Your teeth.

Aleko

           You were my only theme.
I dreamed that between us two I found . . .
O God, the most horrendous dream!

Zemfira

    Don't believe dreams, for they betray us.

Aleko

    I don't believe in anything:
Neither my dreams, nor your sweet prayers,
Nor in the heart you say you bring.

              *

Old Man

    What, you young devil, are you here
Sighing, your head upon your arms?
Here we are free, the skies are clear,
And women famous for their charms.
Weeping unmakes us. What's it for?

Aleko

    She doesn't love me any more.

Old Man

    Listen, my friend: she is a child.
This sorrowing is overdone:
You love with earnestness, beguiled
By women who must love—in fun.
Take heart.

Aleko

             But she was so adoring!
Turning towards me in delight,
In all these lonely places pouring
Her heart out through the hours of night,
So full of childish gaiety!
How often, chattering pell-mell

74

Or with a delirious kiss, did she
Instantaneously dispel
My introspective disposition . . . !
And now, Zemfira, is it farewell . . . ?
Zemfira, why this imposition?

Old Man

Listen: I'll tell you something of
Myself. It is a tale of love . . .
I singled out . . . not long unknown
But long delighted in, a girl
I finally could call my own . . .
Youth quickly gone, quicker therefore
Love's sweet season: in a year
My Mariula loved no more.
Ever since then I've been alone.

Aleko

But it is one thing to condone,
Another to follow there and then
The treacherous girl and thieving men
And stab them straightway to the bone?

Old Man

What for? Youth's freer than a bird
And can't be bridled in its yearning.
Each has his chance. Haven't you heard
That time moves on, is not for turning?

Aleko

I'm not like that. No, my devotion
Will not so easily be lost!
I'll take revenge if I am crossed.

*

Gypsy

Again, again . . . kiss me again.

Zemfira

Enough: I fear his jealousy.

Gypsy

A longer one! A farewell, then.

Zemfira
   He's coming, we must say goodbye.

Gypsy
   And our next meeting?—Tell me when.

Zemfira
   Tonight, at moonrise. Yes, believe me.
   Above the grave beyond the hill . . .

Gypsy
   She will not come! She will deceive me!

Zemfira
   He's here now! Run! . . . I'll come! I will!

                              *

      Aleko slept. His teeming brain
   Played out a morbid fantasy;
   He cried himself awake again,
   Stretching his hand out jealously;
   The hand shrank hesitantly back
   To feel the bedclothes cold—for she
   Was far away . . . and at the lack
   He half-rose, shuddered, listened: he
   Heard nothing. Seized by anxiety,
   Immediate waves of heat and cold
   Assailing him, he left the tent
   To rage, alarming to behold,
   Amongst the wagons; then he went
   Into the silent fields; the moon
   Had long since set; uncertain light
   Of stars on such a misty night
   Lit up the glimmering dew which soon
   Revealed a trail of sorts, which he
   Began to trace impatiently.
   Suddenly he saw two shapes
   And heard a nearby murmuring
   Upon the desecrated slab.

First Voice
   It's time . . .

Second Voice
> Don't go . . .

First Voice
> > It's time, my dear.

Second Voice
> No, no, don't go, let's wait till morning.

First Voice
> It's late as it is.

Second Voice
> > What timid wooing.
> A minute!

First Voice
> > You'll be my undoing.

Second Voice
> One minute!

First Voice
> > What if while I'm here
> My husband wakes up?

Aleko
> > > Do not fear,
> He has. Where are you going now?
> This tomb's appropriate somehow.

Zemfira
> Escape, my love, run quickly . . .

Aleko
> > > > Stay,
> Young monsieur! Whither away?
> Lie there!

(Thrusts a knife into him.)

Zemfira
　　　　　　　Aleko!

Gypsy
　　　　　　　　　I am dying . . .

Zemfira
　　You'll kill him! Look, his blood bespatters
　　You! Aleko, stop it now.
　　What are you doing?

Aleko
　　　　　　　　　　Nothing matters.
　　And least the breath behind your vow.

Zemfira
　　Enough, I am not frightened of
　　Your threats, Aleko, and I spurn
　　Them. For this act I hope you burn . . .

Aleko
　　Die, then, as well!
　　　　　　　　　(*Stabs her.*)

Zemfira
　　　　　　　　　I die in love . . .
　　　　　　　　　*

　　The morning-star, towards the east
　　Glowed in the sky. Beyond the hill
　　Aleko, bloodied like a beast,
　　Sat on the tomb, the knife gripped still
　　Within his fist. Two bodies lay
　　Beside him. He was terrible
　　To look on. The gypsies came, and they
　　Began to crowd shyly around.
　　Women made their weeping way
　　To kiss the dead pair's eyes and say
　　Their prayers; others dug the ground.
　　The lonely father in his place
　　Gazed upon his daughter's face,
　　Silent in grief, with nothing to say.

78

They lifted up the mortal clay
And bore them, side by side, away
And soon the youthful couple lay
In nature's unconcerned embrace.
Aleko watched it all some way
Away, and when the grave was crowned
With its last clod, he toppled prone,
Inert and wordless, from his stone.

Then the old man came up, and spoke.
'Leave us, man of pride! We folk
Are primitive; we have no need
For laws, we do not torture men—
We do not make men groan and bleed—
We will not live with murderers, then . . .
Our life's not yours, since you condone
No liberty except your own.
Such attitudes are our undoing,
Kindly as we are, and shy.
You are too bold. You should be going.
May you perhaps find peace. Goodbye.'

He spoke—and with a general cry
The horde of nomads rose: bereft
Of life this dark vale of the heart,
For in a while the gypsies left
For distant steppes. A single cart
Stood in that fateful meadow (thrown
Across it, one poor rug) alone.
So on occasion, winter dawning,
When at a misty hour of morning
Delayed in their migration, cranes
Rise in great flocks from off the plains
With piercing cries to soar and wind
Southwards in their travelling,
One will sadly stay behind,
Fatally shot, with trailing wing.
Night fell; the wagon stayed unlit,
No one beneath its folded awning
To lay a fire or kindle it,
Or drowse away in sleep till morning.

JO SHAPCOTT

Tales of Ovid

(*from* THE GYPSIES)

A stranger's at the heart of a true story
that does the rounds among us, year on year.
It tells how the Roman emperor exiled
a man from the South, sent him to live with us.
I can't quite bring his name to mind: it was odd.
He was old under his skin, always had been,
but a fragment of soul was young and shivering with life
so that everything he touched turned into song
and his voice was like the sound of rushing water.
And we all loved his company, having him around
on the banks of the Danube, no side to him, no bother.
He charmed us with his stories though his grasp
was tiny about what's what, how to make life tick.
He was a child, helpless and shy, a baby.
Imagine, needing strangers to catch your game
and net and gut your fish, do all your basics.
When the fast river froze itself into stone
and the winds swept in from the north, they covered him—
as smooth as a holy saint he was underneath—
with fluffy fur, rabbit, squirrel and fox.
Small chance he'd take to our poor way of life,
our different worries: hunger, dance and touch.
He wandered around, skin pale and heart dried up,
asking who'd ever listen why the gods
picked him for punishment, how he'd be nothing
until they had a change of heart upstairs.
He grieved out loud, thought warm thoughts about death,
and paced the Danube every daylight minute,
shouted at ice, watched his tears drop, steaming;
yelled words to himself about his home, his city.
Dying he heated up, boiling with words;
he cursed and screamed instructions about his bones
which he swore were pulling south inside him.
They at least should be allowed to leave
to carry some grains of his soul back to the world.

Aleko

(*from* THE GYPSIES)

I called him my little cuckoo,
always on the edge, pushing,
passing through, no nesting instinct,
afraid to get used to anything.
Everywhere, to him, was open road—
even the track of my fingertip
on his skin—everywhere a pillow.
Mornings he'd give the day up to his god
of the moment, hoping that way to stop
the ordinary shocks of life
disturbing his pulse. He liked
to feel a slight lick of fame though;
a little, far-off tingle of success
could be tempting especially when dinners,
parties, the sort of expensive fun
he'd never expected fell into his lap.
He was alone, but he slept on under storms,
rows upstairs, loud flight paths, slept on under
blue quiet ceilings. He knew the fates
were depicted blind, designing,
but he took no more notice
than a finger click, though God knows,
passion had made a trampoline of his soul
and whether he knew it or not,
it was the gods who streamed
through his torso, pinching and scratching at will.
He thought he could control even them.
Your gods always wake up though. Wait.

DANIEL WEISSBORT

Advice

Take it from me . . . When the daily press
Of horseflies and gnats encircles you,
Don't reason, don't waste time on politesses,
On disapproval of that whining crew.
Neither logic nor fancy manners, friend,
Will persuade the pesky race to scram.
Anger they say's a sin—still, stand on end
And slay them with a nifty epigram.

The Georgian Hills

Night swathes the Georgian hills;
    Hard by, the Aragva's roar.
Sad and easy, my sorrow fills,
    Radiant, with you . . .
You. You alone.
             Nothing can tease
    Or trouble my dejectedness one jot.
My heart is smitten, loving yet again,
    Because it is incapable of not.

SEAMUS HEANEY

Arion

We were all hard at it in the boat,
Some of us up tightening sail,
Some down at the heave and haul
Of the rowing benches, deeply cargoed,
Steady keeled, our passage silent,
The helmsman buoyant at the helm;
And I, who took it all for granted,
Sang to the sailors.
                  Then turbulent
Sudden wind, a maelstrom;
The helmsman and the sailors perished.
Only I, still singing, washed
Ashore by the long sea-swell, sing on,
A mystery to my poet self,
And safe and sound beneath a rock shelf
Have spread my wet clothes in the sun.

LOUISE GLÜCK

Omens

I rode to meet you: dreams
like living beings swarmed around me
and the moon on my right side
followed me, burning.

I rode back, everything changed.
My soul in love was sad
and the moon on my left side
trailed me without hope.

To such endless impressions
we poets give ourselves absolutely,
making, in silence, omen of mere event,
until the world reflects the deepest needs of the soul.

RUTH PADEL

Writing to Onegin

Look at the bare wood hand-waxed floor and long
White dressing-gown, the good child's writing-desk
   And passionate cold feet
Summoning music of the night—tumbrils, gongs
And gamelans—with one neat pen, one candle
   Puttering its life out hour by hour. Is 'Tell
Him how I'm feeling' never a good idea? You can't wish
This unlived—this world on fire, on storm
   Alert, till the shepherd's song
Outside, some hyper-active yellowhammer, bulbul,
Wren, amplified in hills and woods, tell her to give
   A spot of notice to the dawn.

'I'm writing to you. Well, that's it, that's everything.
You'll laugh, but you'll pity me too. I'm ashamed of this.
   I meant to keep it quiet. You'd never have known, if—
I wish—I could have seen you once a week. To mull over, day
And night, the things you say, or what we say together.
   But word is, you're misogynist. Laddish. A philanderer
Who says what he doesn't mean. (That's not how you come across
To me.) Who couldn't give a toss for domestic peace—
   Only for celebrity and showing off—
And won't hang round in a provincial zone
Like this. We don't glitter. Though we do,
   Warmly, truly, welcome you.

'Why did you come? I'd never have set
Eyes on a star like you, or blundered up against
   This crazed not-sleeping, hour after hour
In the dark. I might have got the better of
My clumsy fury with constraint, my fret
   For things I lack all lexica and phrase-book art
To say. I might have been a faithful wife; a mother.
But that's all done with. This is Fate. God.
   Sorted. I couldn't give my heart
To anyone else. Here I am—yours, to the last breath.

My life till now has been a theorem, to demonstrate
　　How right it is to love you. This love is love to death.

'I knew you anyway. I loved you, I'm afraid,
In my sleep. Your eyes, that denim-lapis, grey-sea-grey-green
　　Blue, full of anxiety, energy, so much pride,
That Chinese fold of skin at the inner corner, that shot
Look, bleeping "vulnerable" under the screensaver charm,
　　Kept me alive. Every cell, every last gold atom
Of your body, was engraved in me
Already. Don't tell me that was dream! When you came in,
　　Staring round in your stripey coat and brocade
Vest, I nearly died! I fainted, I was flame! I recognised
The you I'd always listened to alone, when I wrote
　　Or tried to wrestle my scatty soul into calm.

'Wasn't it you who slipped through the transparent
Darkness to my bed, whispering love with fine-tuned gusto?
　　Aren't you my guardian angel? Or is this arrant seeming—
A hallucination, thrown
Up by that fly engineering a novel does, so
　　Beguilingly, or poems? Is this mad?
Or are there ways of dreaming I don't know?
Too bad. My soul has made its home
　　In you. I'm here and bare before you: shy,
In tears. But if I didn't heft my whole self up and hold it there—
A crack-free mirror—loving you, or if I couldn't share
　　It, set it out in words, I'd die.

'I'll wait to hear from you. I must.
Please let me hope. Give me one look—from eyes I hardly dare
　　To look back at. Or scupper my dream
By scolding me. I've given you rope
To hang me: tell me I'm mistaken. You're so much in
　　The world; while I just live here, bent on jam
And harvest, songs and books. That's not complaint.
We live such different lives. So—this is the end. It's taken
　　All night. I'm scared to read it back, I'm faint
With shame and fear. But this is what I am.
My crumpled bed, my words, my open self. All I can do is trust
　　The whole damn lot of it to you.'

86

She sighs. The paper trembles as she presses down
The pink wax seal. Outside, the milk mist clears
    From the shimmering valley. If I
Were her guardian angel, I'd divide myself and holler,
Don't! Stay on an even keel! Don't dollop over
    All you are, to a man who'll go to town
On his next little fling. If he's entranced, today,
By the way you finger your silk throat inside your collar,
    Tomorrow there'll be Olga, Sally, Jane. But then I'd whisper
Go for it, petal. Nothing's as real as what you write.
His funeral, if he's not up to it. What we feel
    Is mortal, and won't come again.

So cut, weeks later, to an outside shot: the same girl
Taking cover ('Dear God, he's here, he's come!')
    Under fat red gooseberries, glimmering hairy stars:
The old, rude bushes she has hide-and-seeked in
All her life, where mother commands the serfs to sing
    While picking, so they can't hurl
The odd gog into their mouths. No one could spy
Her here, not even the sun in its burn-time. Her cheeks
    Are simmering fire.
We're talking iridescence, a Red Admiral's last
Tremble before the avid schoolboy plunks his net.
    Or imagine

A leveret—like the hare you shot (remember?)
At the country house—which ran round screaming
    Like a baby? Only mine is shivering, in papery winter corn,
While the hunter (as it might be, you) stomps his Hush
Puppies through dead brush. Everything's quiet.
    She's waited—how long?—ages: stoking pebbly embers
Under the evening samovar, filling
The Chinese teapot—coils of Lapsang Suchong
    Floating to the ceiling in the shadows—tracing O and E
In the window's black reflection, one finger
Tendrilling her own breath on the glass.
    Like putting a shell to your ear to hear the sea

When it's really your own red little sparkle, an echo
Of marching blood. Like she's asking a phantom

World of pearled-up mist for proof
That her man exists: that gamelans and tumbrils
Won't evade her. But now, among the kitchen garden's
    Rose-haws, runaway mallow and Pernod-
Coloured pears, she unhooks herself thorn by thorn
For the exit aria. For fade-out. Suddenly, there he is
    In the avenue—the man she's written to! Charon
Gazing at her with flaming eyes; Darth Vader
From *Star Wars*! She's trapped—in a house she didn't realise
    Was blazing. Her letter was a gate to the inferno.

PATRICIA BEER

Raven to Raven

Raven to raven wheels
Raven to raven calls:
What shall we eat today?
Where shall we find our prey?

Raven to mate replies:
I know when someone dies.
Down in that willowy field
A knight is lying killed.

Who did it and why?
Nobody can reply
Except his falcon, his black steed
And his young bride.

His bird has flown off course
The killer rides his horse
His widow will await
A living mate.

To the Tsar Nicholas I

As Tsar he lost no time
In punishing what he called crime.
He exiled a hundred and twenty men straightway
And hanged five the next day.

To I. I. Pushchin

My earliest friend, the friend whom I can trust,
I recall exile and the joy I felt
On hearing sleigh bells—knowing that they must
Be yours—enter my courtyard, which was just
Filling up with snow that would not melt.

I pray to God the poem that I send
Now that you are condemned by the same rule
May give you comfort too, my closest friend,
And shed on you from this day to the end
The light that used to shine on us at school.

The Poet

Until Apollo visits him
The poet is as good as dead.
His mind has shrunk, his sight is dim.
A petty world pervades his head.
His precious lyre has broken down.
With soul asleep beyond recall
Of all the feeble men in town
He is the feeblest of them all.

But when at last Apollo speaks
To someone who can now reply,
Just like an eagle when it wakes
The poet grooms his wings to fly.
He cannot bear the world at play.
Their chattering he cannot stand.
He will not honour or obey
Even the greatest in the land.
And so he runs off gracelessly,
Compulsively, he has no choice,
Towards an empty, silent sea
And woods that do not raise their voice.

'Please God, let me not lose my mind'

Please God, let me not lose my mind
For I would rather be a pilgrim
    Or a poor working lad
Not because I set much store
On sanity. In fact I could
    Cheerfully go mad.

If they would only let me be
Gladly I would at once seek out
    Some group of shadowy trees
And sing with crazy vehemence
Abandoning myself to nights
    Of glorious fantasies.

And I would listen to the sea
And I would look up with delight
    Into a hollow sky
I would be fierce I would be free
A hurricane uprooting fields
    And making forests lie.

There is a snag: you lose your wits
And people shun you like the pox
    And lock you in a cell.
Lunatics are put in chains.
And creatures indescribable
    Will come to give you hell.

And after dark I should not hear
The singing of the nightingale
    Nor any rustling leaf
But my fellow inmates screaming
And the wardens' night shift swearing.
Clanking chains. And grief.

André Chénier

DEDICATED TO N. N. RAEVSKY

While the awestruck crowds stand gaping
With respect at Byron's tomb
And the lyres of Europe praise him
His ghost joins Dante's in the gloom.

Silent in dying and in death
Another ghost means more to me,
One who was, thirty years ago,
Killed in the name of Liberty.

He sang of nature, love and peace.
I take him flowers, and music too:
A new lyre has struck up for him.
He hears my song and so do you.

ELAINE FEINSTEIN

Exegi Monumentum

I've set up for myself a monument, though not in stone.
No hands have made it, and no weeds will grow
Along the path to where the stubborn
    Head soars above Alexander's column.

I shall not die altogether. Lyrics of mine,
Although my flesh decays, will hold my spirit
And I'll be known as long as any poet
    Remains alive under the moon.

News of me then will cross the whole of Russia
And every tribe there will have heard my name:
The Slavs, the Finns, and those in the wild Tungus,
    The Kalmucks on the plain.

And they will all love me, because my songs
Evoked some kindness in a cruel age,
Since I once begged for mercy to assuage
    The wrongs of the downfallen.

So, Muse, obey God's orders without fear,
Forget insults, expect no laurel wreaths;
Treat praise and slander with indifference.
    And never argue with a fool.

INDEX OF PUSHKIN POEMS

The original titles or first lines of Pushkin's poems which inspired the poetry contained in this volume are given on the left. Below them, where necessary, are their literal English translations. On the right are the titles or first lines of the poems collected here, with page references.